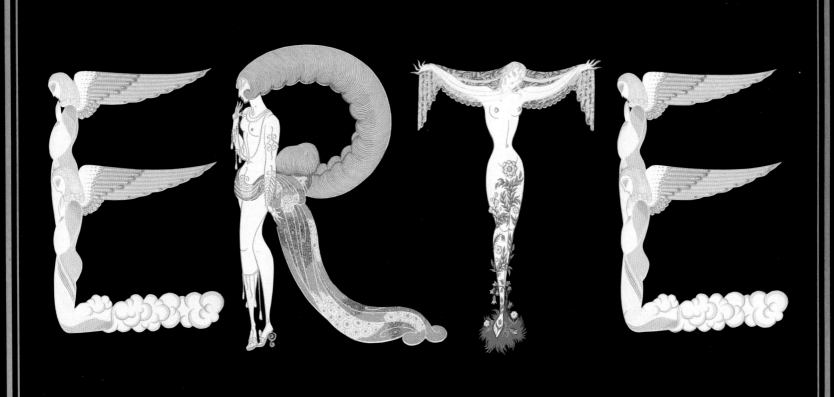

CONTENTS

My reminiscences of Erté

Erté and me: a twenty-five year relationship.

Erté was family to me and my wife Salomé who died last year; when my grandson was born he became a Godfather.

My wife and I looked after his business affairs for twenty-five years but she was a designer as well, so she worked closely with him on the creative side.They had an almost telepathic communication. They needed hardly any explanation on any subject.

The French art dealer Jâcques Damèse introduced us to Erté because we owned a gallery where we had relaunched the career of Alphonse Mucha, the so-called father of Art Nouveau. When it was suggested I meet him, I was really interested. It seemed the timing was perfect to relaunch Erté, the so-called leader of Art Déco, after our success with Mucha in Art Nouveau. This was the beginning of a relationship with Erté that was to last over twenty-five years, but not just as a business partner; he grew so close we became his new family.

We had no sooner met him than we were planning his exhibition and then holding his solo showings at our Grosvenor galleries in New York and London. It was a remarkable success that the New York Metropolitan Museum bought all 170 of his works and next year, 1968, the Metropolitan held the exhibition "Erté and contemporaries". Other artists were included in the same showing because in those days the Met. had a policy of not doing solo showings of living artists. This exhibition was mainly of his costume designs. A few years later the Met. held an exhibition of only Francis Bacon's work; so I reckon Erté's gave rise to a new approach to 20 th century art at the Metropolitan and helped change its policy.

When Erté moved to Paris his cousin came from Russia and looked after his business affairs, but when the cousin died it seems Erté had to look after his business alone. Now, no artist is gifted when it comes to business and Erté was no exception, so we established "Sevenarts Limited" and took charge of his business affairs.

His own collection of his work began around 1910-1911 either just before he came to Paris to study Illustration or in Paris with the sketches he drew for a Russian fashion magazine in 1912.

His career as a costume designer started when Paul Poiret, himself a costume designer in Paris, approved him and employed him as his production designer. Erté wasn't even twenty-one, so his father, an Admiral in pre-revolution Russia had to come to Paris to sign the contract. All the costume sketches for Poiret were duly filed. The most admirable thing was that Erté kept all his work, he didn't even rip up the ones he didn't like; like a squirrel hoarding nuts for winter. Around 1965-1966 I sorted out all the originals from the 21,000 works in his collection. One big problem now is that there are so many unoriginal works everywhere. We get a good idea of his meticulous nature from the way he kept his collection. He had the same attitude towards his daily schedule: almost stereotyped, except when he was no holiday. He would always sit at his dest, starting work late in the evening and not putting down his pen until the early mornig. His partners for this routine were his two cats who would spend the night curled up on the desk or around his feet. With classical music playing in his workroom; this time of creativity was the happiest for him. He had been spending summer in Majorca for twenty or thirty years. I don't know why Majorca, but after his first holiday after World War II, Majorca always seemed to have a special place in his heart. At the beginning he stayed in a small hotel, a room with a balcony and the perople in the hotel were very kind; later they built him an annexed house and always gave him a marvellous reception.

Our meeting him was a turning point because it allowed him to realise his dream. It was important to him to have his own house and land. He enjoyed his life on that island and had his daily schedule, which was, after breakfast, to go down the slope to the beach to swim and sunbathe. He was a sun-worshipper and watching him playing with the waves, the sun shining and the sea shimmering blue he looked like a small child brimming over with happiness. He did an abstract sculpture a few years ago; the inspiration came while he was laying on the sand sunbathing in Majorca. The sun had always played an important part in Erté's imagination and creative energy. The Sixties was the best time when considering Erté's work, we can't think otherwise. Before 1960 a distinct line was drawn between decorative artists and fine artists; especially in America where artists such as Erté were thought of as decorative painters. The Sixties was the time when classification such as this became nonsense. The typical example is Andy Warhol. He made people in the art world accept graphics as an art form: the concept of art itself changed in America. After World War II, we observed another new phenomenon: the Bourgeoisie started to collect art. People who had not had an interest besides their own Businesses suddenly became collectors. This new crop of collectors was a lucky phenomenon for the museums too, because they didn't only collect but contribute to museums. They got their names put up next to the painting displayed, mainly to satisfy their pride. In the States where people couldn't obtain titles of nobility it became a symbol of power.

Erté's name became world-famous when he achieved great commercial success with his "Alphabet" lithographs. I remember he did the "Alphabet" work in the Twenties. At the time I was promoting an exhibition in London, so we loaned the "Alphabet" work belonging to art collectors Lord and Lady Beaumont. I had received requests from many people wanting "Alphabet" works done in their own names. We negotiated with Lord and Lady Beaumont and bought it back for several times the original price. But it prove to be a far-sighted and wise action as we made many variations of the plate it was based on and we started to make lithographs. My idea, by the way.

He followed the big success of "Alphabet" with further successes; "Number", "Four Seasons" and "Ace of Trumps". The lithograph has made it possible to hold exhibitions at many different museums and galleries. The name of Erté has now spread world-wide and it has brought us success beyond our wildest imaginings. The staff at Chalk and Vermilion Fine Arts Ltd. who were in charge of Erté's graphical work spared nothing in trying out new methods, materials and colour contrasts for the transformation of his works into 3-D. It was also a great discovery for him to see the wonderful effect of the lithographs that lost none of the essential Erté.

He was extremely thrilled with the 3-D effect on his first seriograph printed in 1974. Then in the eighties he became involved with producing bronze figures, clearly the interpretation of his own illustrations that had appeared in "Harper's Bazaar" for nearly twenty years. Working in new material like clay excited and impressed him because it was a totally new experience for him to have the particular feeling from using clay and making up bronze figures. I still just can't accept the fact that he's no longer with us. I've never known anyone like him who can enjoy life so much and keep the spirit of youthfulness. There was always something to come. I had believed he was perennial, but at least his lifetime's creations really are immortal. This thought is my only consolation.

On the 13th August I visited Eric Estorick, Chairman of "Sevenarts Limited", while he was staying at an hotel in New York on business. He was able to spare more than the thirty minutes I had expected, to give me a retrospective of the twenty-five years he knew Erté. When his long reminiscence was over he added that he was looking forward to visiting Japan for the opening of the exhibition of Erté's work in October, but it made him sad to think of the Japanese admirers without Erté there to meet them.

Profile

1892: Romain de Tirtoff, son of an admiral, born in St. Petersburg, Russia

1898: Designs a dress for his mother that she has made into a ballgown.

1900: Visits World's Fair in Paris with his mother and sister. Decides he wants to live there someday.

1906: Studies painting with portraitist Ilya Repin.

1912: His parents consent to let him study art in Paris.Studies at Académie Julian with historical painter Jean-Paul Laurens, but dislikes the regimented structure of classes and leaves after several months to become a fashion designer. Contributes sketches to Russsian fashion magazine Damsky Mir.

1913: Works for one monthe with the dressmaker Caroline. She tells him he has no talent for designing. He then submits fashion sketches to Paul Poiret. Poiret recognizes his talent and hires him as one of two full-time designers. Creates costumes for his first theatrical production, Le Minaret, featuring Mata Hari. Contributes drawings to La Gazette du Bon Ton, leading fashion magazine of Paris. First use of signature "Erté."

1914: Poiret closes because of war. Erté designs for Henri Bendel and Altman's in New York. Submits designs to Harper's Bazar.

1915: Harper's Bazar publishes first cover design (January) and designs on interior pages, beginning a twenty-two-year collaboration.

1916: Erté contributes work to Vogue magazine. After six months, Willam Randolph Hearst, owner of Harper's Bazar, signs ten-year exclusive contract with Erté to prevent him from creating more designs for Vogue. First costume and set designs for a music hall: Madame Rasmini's Théâtre Bataclan in Paris.

1917: Creates costumes for revue, Marvels of the Orient, starring Maurice Chevalier and Mistinguett at Théâtre Femina, Paris.

1919: Designs costumes for Gaby Deslys, Théâtre Femina. First designs for Folies-Bergère. Works with Max Weldy, head of Folies-Bergère costume workshop, and thoroughly learns architecture of theater and mechanics of stage. Will continue costume and set designs for Folies-Bergère for eleven years.

1920: Costumes for Ganna Walska of Chicago Opera Company for La Bohème, I Pagliacci, and Faust, among others. Costumes for Mary Garden of Chicago Opera Company for L'Amore dei Tre Re. His costume designs used in film Restless sex, starring Marion Davies (Cosmopolitan Films). Exhibition at Knoedler Gallery, New York.

1921: Costume designs for Anna Pavlova.

1922: Costum and set designs for George White's Scandals, Irving Berlin's Music Box Revue, and Winter Garden in New York. Costume designs for Ganna Walska in Rigoletto at Paris Opera.

1923: Costume and set designs for Ziegfeld Follies, New York. Illustrations for La Gazette du Bon Ton. Fashion drawings for Ladies' Home Journal.

1924: Costume designs for Le Secret du Sphinx by Maurice Rostand at Théâtre Sarah Bernhardt, Paris. Illustrations for The Sketch, London, and Ladies' Home Journal.

1925: Goes to Hollywood, under constract to Metro-Goldwyn-Mayer, to design sets and costumes for film Paris. Costume and set designs for George White's Scandals. Exhibition at Madison Gallery, New York. Paris producttion delayed, and Erté designs costumes for other films, The Mystic, Dance Madness, A Little Bit of Broadway, and King Vidor's La Bohème, starring Lillian Gish.

1926: Returns to France, dissatisfied with caricature the producers of Paris have created. Makes cover designs and illustrations for Paris magazine Art et Industrie. Singns second ten-year contract with Harper's Bazar. Costume and set designs for Geoge White's Scandals and Folies-Bergère.

1927: Costume designs for Lucrezia Bori in Pelléas et Mélisannde, L' Amore dei Tre Re, and Les Contes d'Hoffmann at Metropolitan Opera, Costume and set designs for Geoge White's musical comedy Manhattan Mary at Majestic Theater, New York. Echibition at Studio Gallery, Brussels.

1929: Article and illustrations for The Encyclopaedia Britannica (14th ed.) Costume and set designs for La Princesse Lointaine by Edomond Rostand at Théâtre Sarah Bernhardt. Exhibition at Galerie Charpentier, Paris, and William Fox Gallery, New York. Illustrations for International Cosmopolitan and The Sketch. Collection of fabric designs for Amalgamated Silk Corporation, New York.

1930: Second collection of fabric designs for Amalgamated Silk. Illustrations for Art Industrie, International Cosmopolitan, and The

Sketch.

1931: Costume and set designs for Folies–Bergére. Costume designs for Ganna Walska in Pelléas et Mélisande (Chicago Opera Company).

1932: Set designs for Faust and Don Pasquale at Riga Opera.

1933: Designs for Bal Tabarin, Paris.

1934: Costume and set designs for Au Temps des Merveilleuses at Théâtre du Châtelet, Paris. Costume designs for Les Travaux d' Hercule, operetta by Claude Terrasse at Théâtre des Capucines, Paris. Exhibition at Waldorf-Astoria Hotel, New York.

1935: Costume and set designs for Théâtre Alhambra and Bal Tabarin, Paris, and French Casino, New York.

1937: Costume and set designs for Plaisir de France, Bal Tabarin; It's in the Bag, by Cecil Landeau, Saville Theatre, London; and Scala Theatre, Berlin. Resigns from Harper's Bazaar in dispute with editor Carmel Snow.

1938: Costume and set designs for London Symphony, Palladium, and Fleet's Lit Up, Hippodrome, London.

1939: Costume and set designs for George White's show at San Francisco Exposition. Costume and set designs for Un Vrai Paradis, Bal Tabarin, and Black Velvet, Palladium, London.

1942: Costume and set designs for lecocq's operetta, Les Cent Vierges, Théâtre–del' Apollo, Paris; Lido, Paris; and André Messager's operetta, Coupe de Roulis, Theatre Marigny, Paris.

1943: Costume and set designs for Van Parys's operetta, Une Femme par Jour, Théâtre des Capucines; Belamour, Théâtres des Nouveautés; Lido; and Bal Tabarin; all Paris. Decoration of windows of Au Printemps department store, Paris.

1945: Costume and set designs for Rossini's The Barber of Seville for French television, Costume and set designs for Lido and Bal Tabarin.

1947: Costume and set designs for Frencis Poulenc's opera Les Mamelles de Tirésias, at Opéra-Comique,Paris. Costume and set designs for Bal Tabarin, and a revue at Opera House, Blackpool.

1948: Costume and set designs for Maurice Ravel's ballet Ma Mère l' Oye, at Opéra-Comique, Paris, and Sueños de Vlena at Teatro Comico, Barcelona.

1949: Costume and set designs for Puss in Boots at Palladium, London.

1951: Costume and set designs for La Traviata, Paris Opera; Fancy Free, Prince of Wales Theatre, London; Histoires d'Eve, La Nouvelle Eve, Paris; Happy Go Lucky, Opera House, Blackpool; and La Leçond' Amour dans un Parc, a musical comedy by Guy Lafarge at Théâtre des Bouffes Parisiens.

1952: Costume and set designs for Pelléas et Mélisande and Albert Roussel's Padmavâti, at Teatro San Carlo, Naples; Mozart's Cosi fan Tutti, Opéra-Comique, Paris; Ring Out the Bells, Victoria Palace, London; Bet Your Life, Hippodrome, London; and Les Filles d'Eve, at La Nouvelle Eve. Costume and set designs for Maske in Blau for Bavaria-Films, Munich.

1953: Costume designs for Die Geschiedene Frau, for Bavaria-Films. Costume and set designs for Caccia al Tesoro, Teatro delle Quattro Fontane, Rome.

1955: Costume and set designs for Jacques Ibert's opera, Gonzague, at Cannes and Rouen opera houses; Campañas de Vena, Teatro Comico, Barcelona; and La Plume de Ma Tante, Garrick Theatre, London.

1957: Costume and set designs for Richard Strauss's Capriccio, Opéra–Comique, and Pommes à l'Anglaise, Théâtre de Paris.

1958: Costume and set designs for Massenet's opera, Don Cezar de Bazan, Rouen Opera; La Plume de Ma Tante, Royal Theatre, New York; and revues at Drap d'Or and Folies-Pigalle, Paris.

1959: Costume and set designs for Donizetti's Don Pasquale, Opéra-Comique, Paris, and Crown Jewels, Victoria Palace, London.

1960: Costume and set designs for Racine's Phèdre, Théâtre du Vieux Colombier, Paris; set designs for Robert Thomas's Piège pour un Homne Seul. Théâtre des Bouffes Parisiens. Costume and set designs for ballet films of Louis Cuny: Le Coiffeur-Miracle and Èdition Speciale.

1961: Costume and set designs for Rameau's Castor et Pollux, Théâtre Antique de Fourvières, Lyons Festival and Moulin Rouge, Paris. Set designs for Olé, Deutschlandshalle, West Berlin.

1963: Costume and set designs for Latin Quarter, New York.

1964: Costumu and set designs for Woderworld, New York's World's Fair; Terence's The Eunuch, Comédie de Paris; and Latin Quarter, New York. Exhibition of Formes Picturales (metal sheet sculpture decorated with oil pigment) at Galerie Ror Volmar,

Paris.

1965: Exhibitions at Galerie Motte, Paris, and Galleria Milano, Milan.

1966: Exhibition, "Les Années 25", at Musée des Arts Décoratifs, Paris, commemorating 1925 exhibition that marked emergence of Art Deco movement. Exhibition at Galerie Jacques Perrin, Paris, and "100 Years of Harper's Bazaar", New York.

1967: Costume and set designs for "Flying Colors", Expo'67, Montreal. Exhibition at Grosvenor Gallery, New York; this entire exhibition of 170 works was purchased by Metropolitan Museum of Art, New York. Exhibition at Grosvenor Galley, London, with numerous works purchased by Victoria and Albert Museum. Exhibition at Galerie Jacques Perrin, Paris; Viotti, Turrin; and Galleria d'Arte Cavalletto, Bresca.

1968: Costume designs for The Silent Night, a ballet for television, New York. First lithographs, The Numerals, published by Grosvenor Gallery. Exhibitions at Metropolitan Museum of Art; Neues Kunst –Zen–trum, Hamburg; Galleria Paolo Barozzi, Venice.

1969: Illustrations for two books, Ermyntrude, and Esmeralda, by Lytton Strachey, and The Beatles Illustrated. Exhibition at Galerie René Drouet.

1970: Awarded title "Chevalier du Mérite, Artisique et Culturel" by French govenment. Costume and set designs for Zizi Jeanmaire Show, produced by Roland Petit, Casino de Paris. Exhibition at Galeria Arvil, Mexico City.

1971: Exhibitions at Galleria della Rocchetta, Parma; Galleria Marino, Rome; Galerie Proscenium, Paris; and Club dei Bibliofili of Milan, Bologna, and Palermo.

1972: Costume and set designs for Zizi, Je T'Aime, produced by Roland Petit, Casino de Paris. Exhibition at Rizzoli Gallery, New York.

1974: Creates Splendeur, his first serigraph. This begins collaboration with Circle Fine Art as his publisher of prints. Exhibition at Galerie Proscenium, Paris. Costume and set designs for Ragtime Ballet, Ballet Théâtre, Angers. Poster designs for Alcazar nightclub and Folies–Bergère.

1975: Costume designs for Schéhérazade, produced by Robert Hossein. Publication of autobiography, Things I Remember.

1976: Awarded title "Officer of Arts and Letters." by French government. Exhibition at Shiseido Gallery, Tokyo.

1977: Honored with Ziegfeld Award of Excellence at the Ziegfeld Ball, New York. Publication of The Alphabet portfolio, combinig lithography and serigraphy. Graphics restrospective exhibition at Circle Galleries, New York, Los Angeles, San Francisco, San Diego, Chicago; Gallery in the Square, Boston; and Cherry Creek Gallery of Fine Art, Denver.

1978: Honored by Eugene O'Neill Foundation at gala "Broadway's in Fashion" celebration, New York, CBS-TV film on Erté, narrated by Diana Vreeland. Exhibition of Erte costumes for New York's Latin Quarter, Boston Center for the Arts.

1979: French documentary, Erté–Or a Magician in the Twentieth Century, released. Smithsonian Institution organizes traveling retrospective exhibition that tours the United States, Canada, and Mexico for three years.

1980: Cosutume and set designs for Glyndebourne Opera Company's perfomance of Der Rosenkavalier.

1982: Major Erté exhibition in Copenhagen, Denmark. Awarded Médaille de Vermeil de la Ville de Paris.

1983: Collaborated on a musical autobiography, Erté Participated in designing a collection of women's haute couture clothing and millinery.

1984: Designed Christmas packaging for a Swiss hosiery company. Created new posters for Folies–Bergère and Campari.

1985: Costume and set designs for Arthur Schnitzler's Anatol, premiering in Los Angeles. Awarded the Legion of Honor by France.

1986: Commission to design cover of January 1987 Playboy magazine. Commission to design offical poster for new Theatre Museum, London. Commission to design a bottle for Courvoisier cognác. Retrospective exhbition Boulogne–Billancourt (Paris), "75 Ans de Creation, 1918–1986". Ninety–fourth birthday exhibition, Grosvenor Gallery, London.

1989: Selected as an honorable member of the American Illustrators' Society (63 members including Norman Rockwell). Awarded the title of honorable doctor by the Royal College of Art

1990: Dies on April 21.

THE GRAPHICS

1

2

THE ACES

1. Diamond/1974
2. Heart/1974
3. Spade/1974
4. Club/1974

3

4

THE NUMERALS
5. 「0」/1980

6. 「1」/1980

7. 「2」/1980

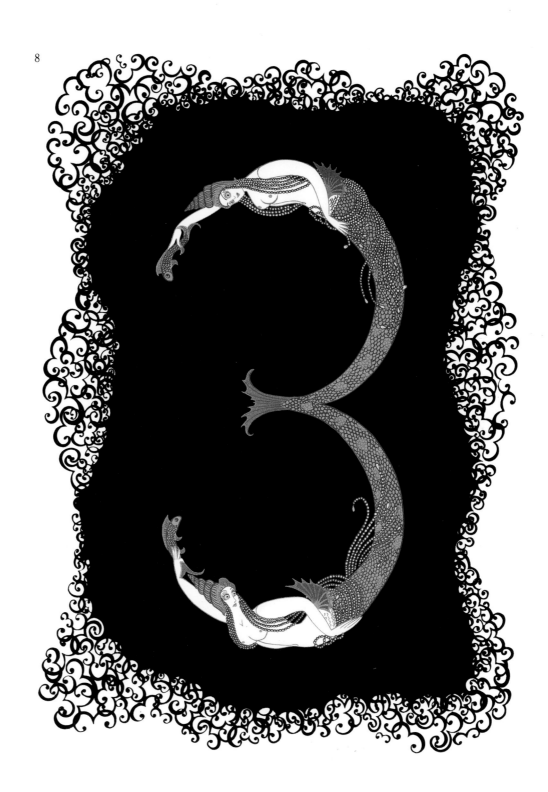

8.　「3」/1980

9

9.「4」/1980

10. 「5」/1980

11. 「6」/1980

12. 「7」/1980

13. 「8」/1980

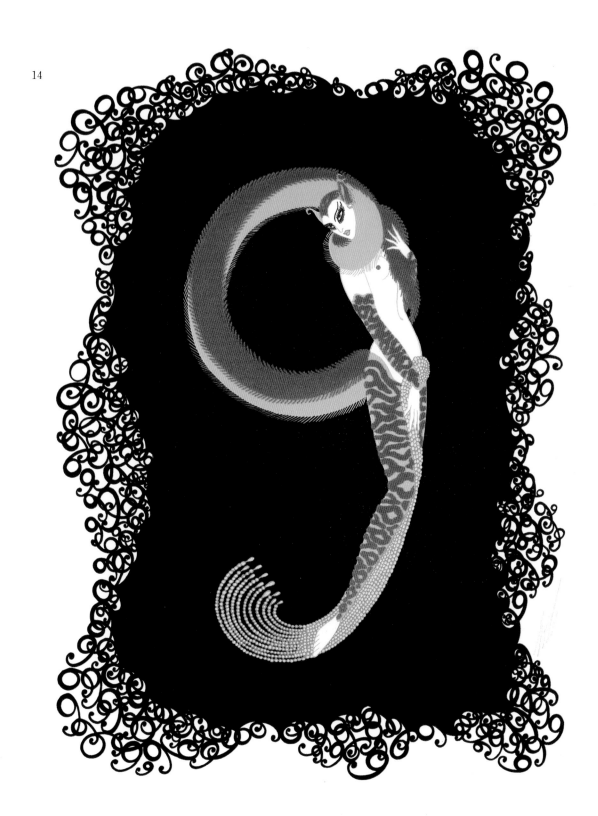

14. 「9」/1980

15

16

THE ALPHABET
15. 「A」/1976
16. 「B」/1976

17. 「C」/1976
18. 「D」/1976

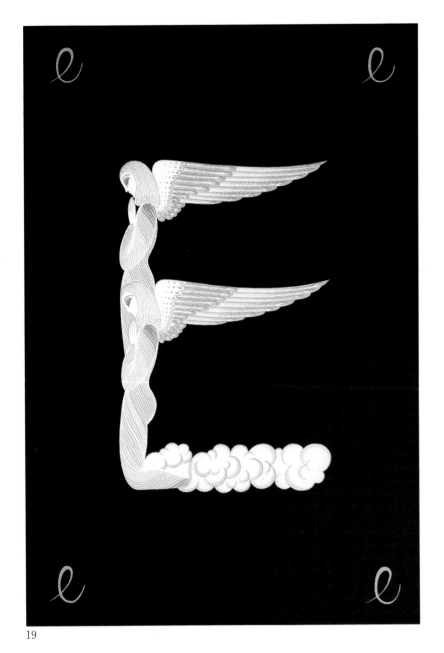

19

20

19. 「E」/1976
20. 「F」/1976

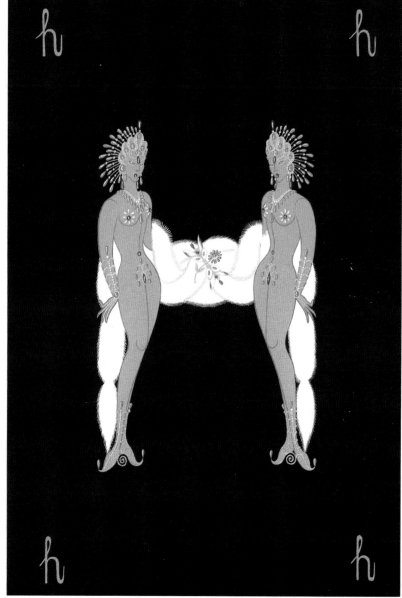

21

22

21.　「G」/1976
22.　「H」/1976

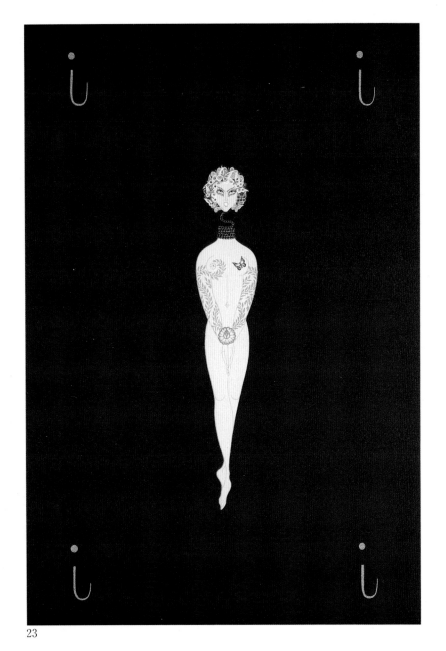

23

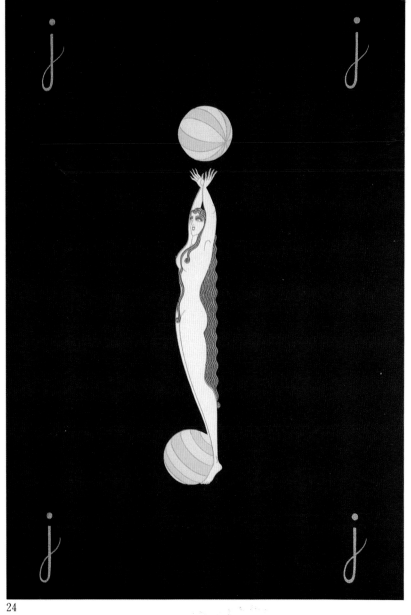

24

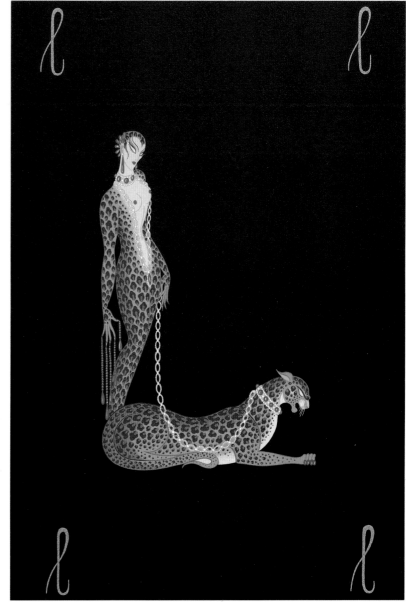

25

26

25. 「K」/1977
26. 「L」/1977

27

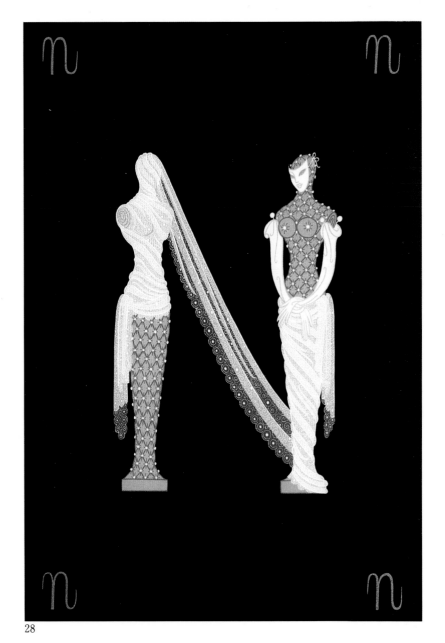

28

27. 「M」/1977
28. 「N」/1977

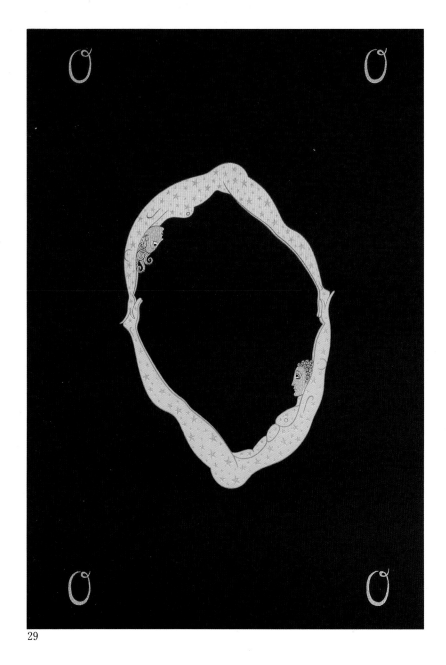

29

30

29.　「O」/1976
30.　「P」/1977

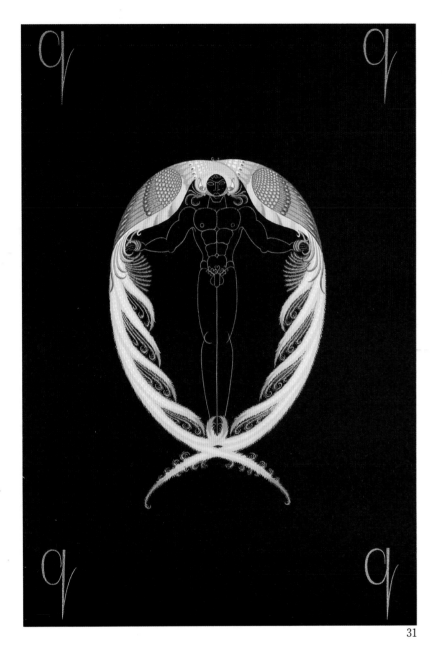

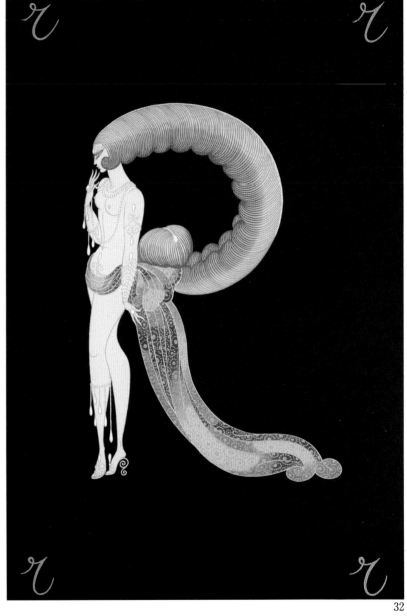

32. 「R」/1977

32

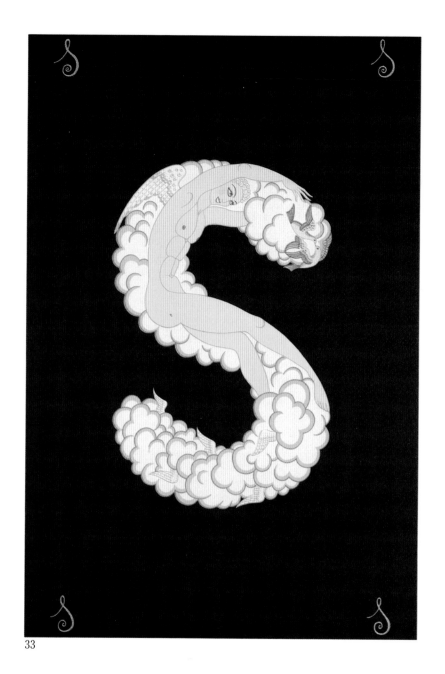

33

34

33.　「S」/1977
34.　「T」/1977

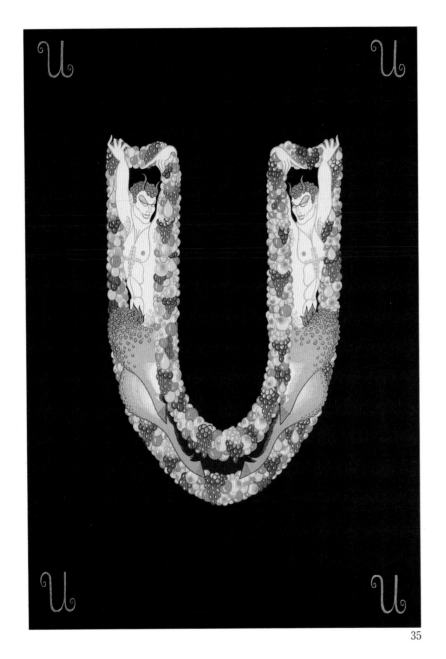

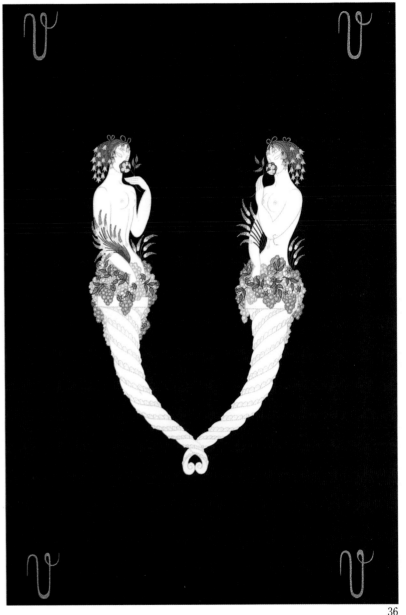

35. 「U」/1977
36. 「V」/1977

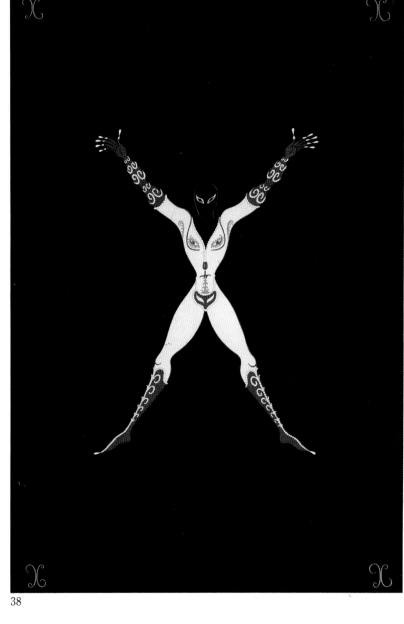

37

38

37. 「W」/1977
38. 「X」/1977

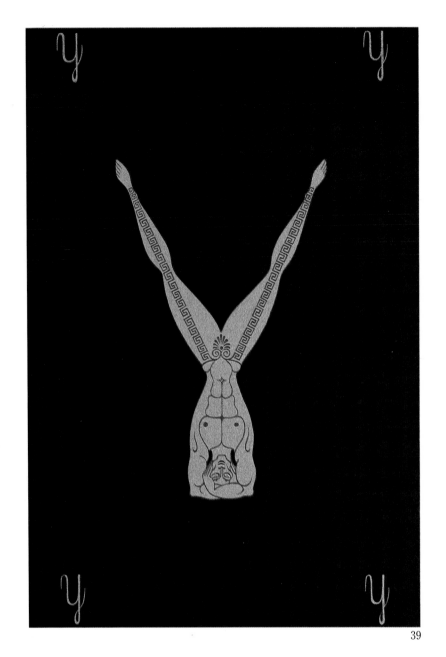

39

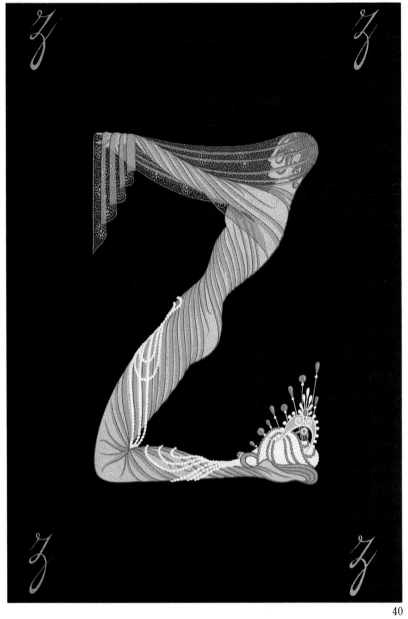

40

39. 「Y」/1977
40. 「Z」/1977

41

42

VANPS

41. La Pretentieuse/1979
42. Black Magic/1979

43

44

43. Circe/1979

44. Seductress/1979

45. L'Empanachée/1979
46. Temptress/1979

THE TWENTIES REMEMBERED
47. Les Jolies Dames/1977

48. Beauty and the Beast/1977

49

50. Openning Night/1985

**MORNING,DAY,
EVENING,NIGHT,SUITE**
51.Morning,Day/1985

52. Evening, Night / 1985

JUNE BRIDES SUITE
53. Fringe Gown/1985

54. Veil Gown/1985

55. Manhattan Mary II/1979

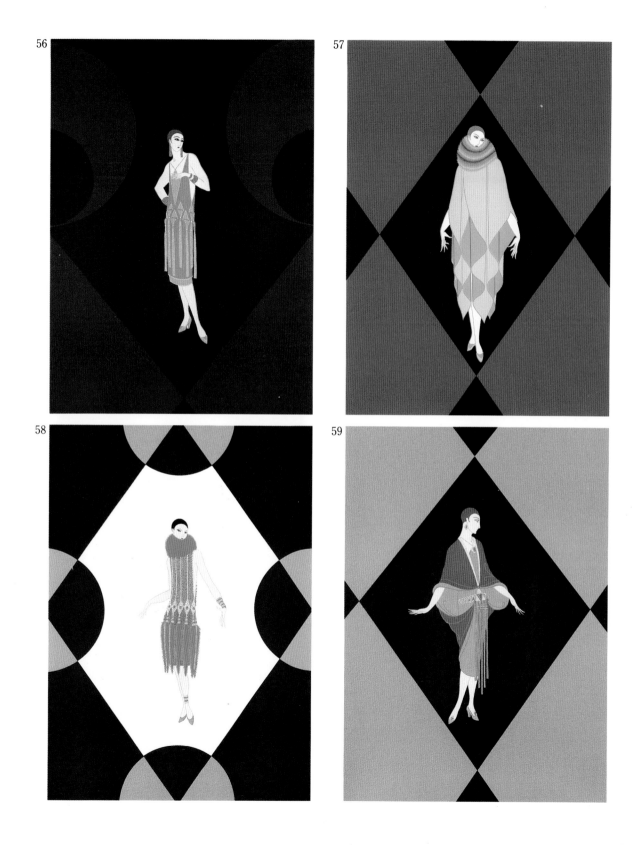

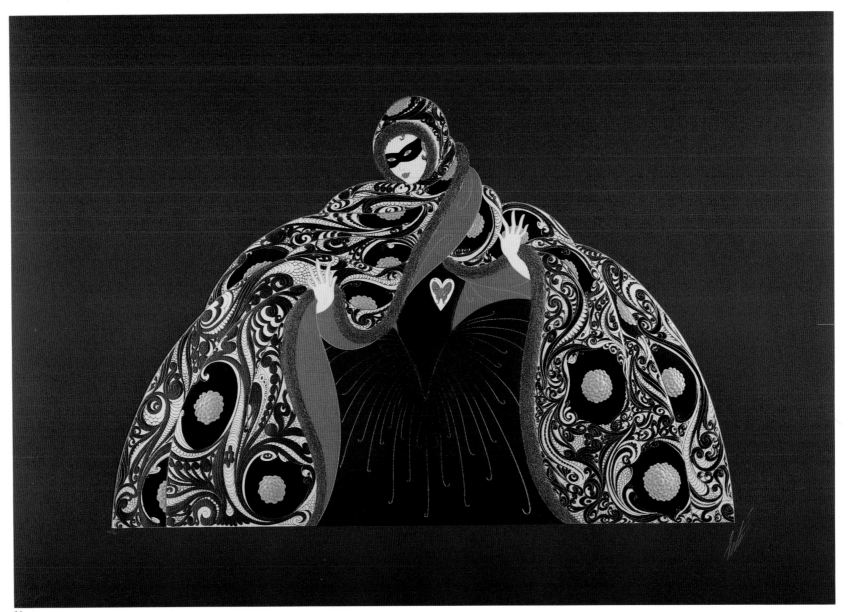

MASQUERADE

60. Masquerade I /1987

61. Masquerade II/1987

**PARIS DAY AND
NIGHT SUITE**
62．Faubourg　St.Honre/1987

63. Place de l'Opéra/1987

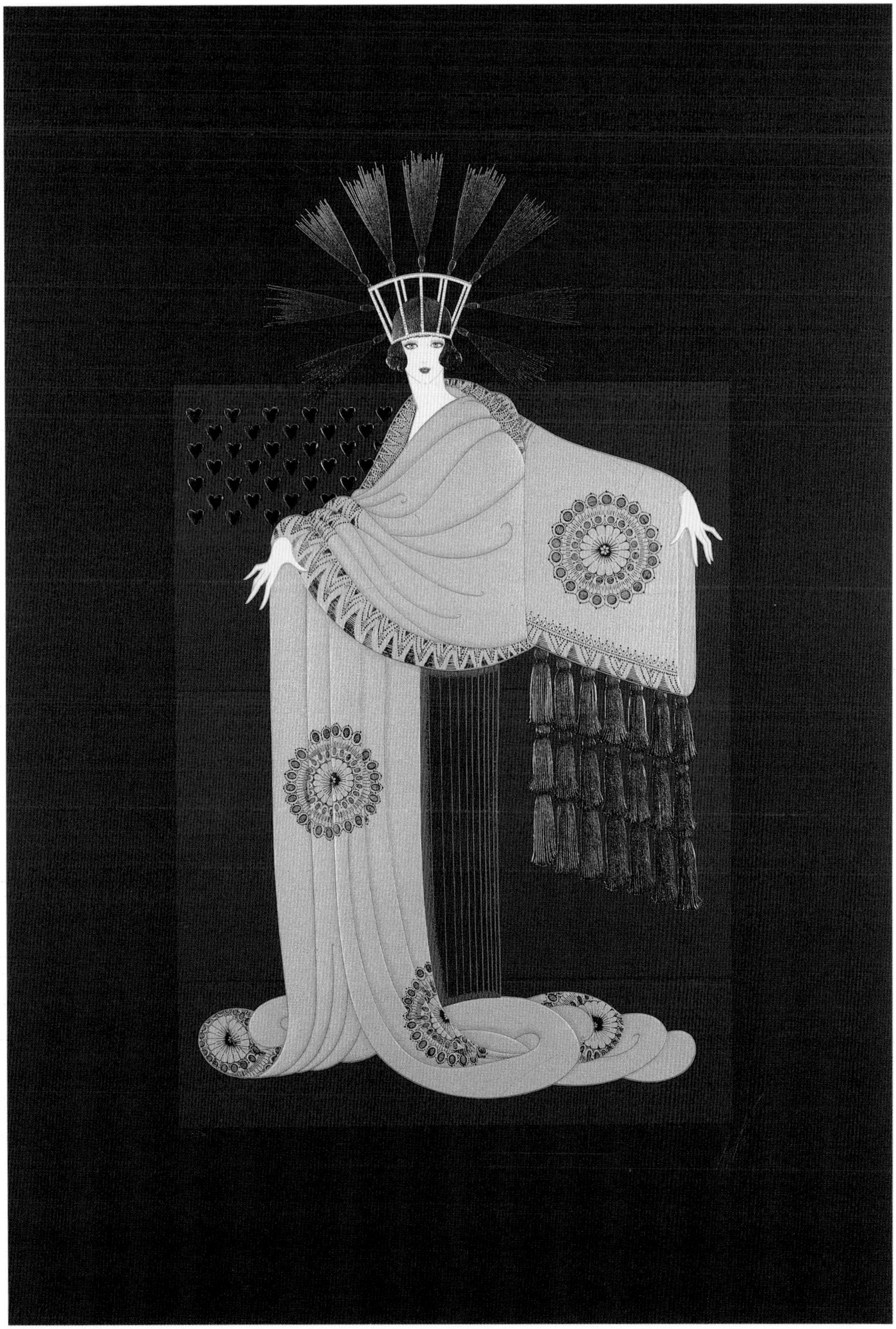

THE AMERICAN
MILLIONAIRESS SUITE
64. Tassel Gown/1987

65. Fringe Cape/1987

66. Mother of Pearl/1987

67. Devotion/1987

68. Moon Garden/1987

69. A Dream/1987

70. Ermine Brocade/1987

71. Haute Couture/1987

72.Gara/1987

73. The Harvest/1987

74. Ladies in Waiting/1987

75. Arabian Nights/1987

76. The Necklase/1987

77. Bacchante/1987

78. Lilies and Lace/1987

79

79. Black Rose/1975

80

83

113/260

81

82

80. Yvette/1975
81. Simone/1975
82. Renée/1975
83. Nicole/1975

84

85

84. Bon Sir/1975
85. Premier/1975

86

87

88

89

86. The Veil/1975
87. Feathers/1975
88. Summer and
    Winter/1975
89. The Kiss/1975

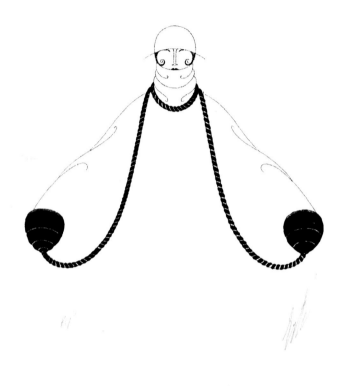

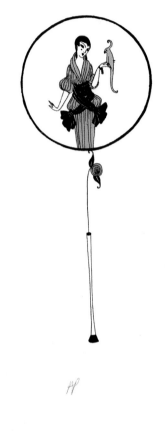

90

91

90. Ficelle/1976
91. Fantaisie/1976

92. Summer Breeze/1978

93. Flames of Love/1978

94. Fall/1979

95. The Mirror/1979

96. Gaby Deslys/1979

97. The Golden Cloack/1979

98. Dinarzade/1979

99. Zobeide/1979

100. Bagdad/1979

101. King's Favorite/1979

102. Woman and Satyr/1980

103. Paresseuse/1980

104. Vintage/1980

105 . Heat/1980

106. Michelle/1980

107

108

107. The Wave/1980
108. Noon/1980

109

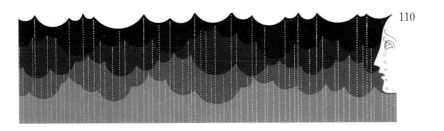

110

109. Lady with a Rose/1980
110. Rain/1980

111

111. Twin Sisters/1981

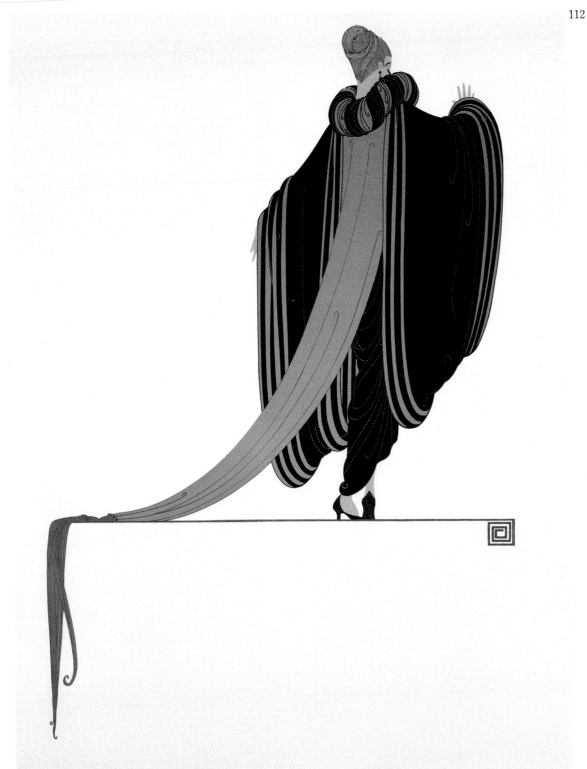

112. Ready for the Ball/1981

113. Ready for the Ball/1981

XXII/CXII

114. Cloudy Morning/1981

115. The Duel/1981

116. The Bubbles/1981

117. Gala Performance/1981

118. Applause/1981

119. The Coming of Spring /1981

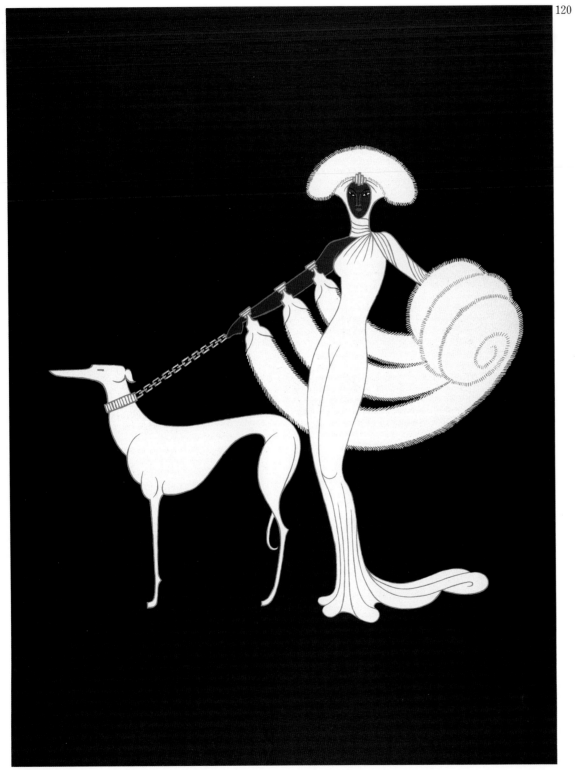

120. Ebony and White/1982

121

122

121. The Surprises of the Sea/1982
122. Writer in Landscape/1982

123

123. The Angel/1983

124

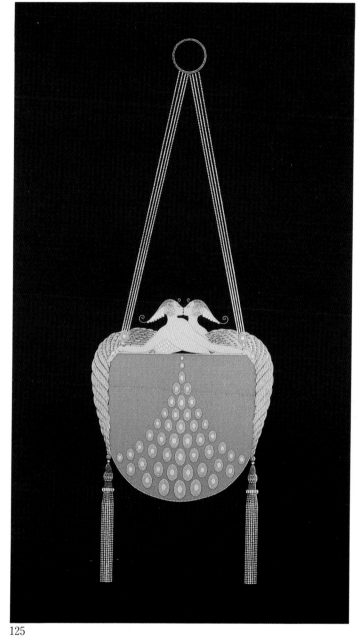

125

124.Columbine/1983
125.The Clasp/1983

126. Loge de Théâter/1984

127

128

127. Moonlight/1984
128. Sunrise/1984

129. Emerald Eyes/1985

130. Aphrodite/1985

131. Feather Gown/1985

132. Pillow Sing/1985

133. Rigoletto/1985

134. The Mirror/1985

135. The Contessa/1985

136. Three Graces/1985

137. The Pursuite of Flore/1985

138. Glamour / 1985

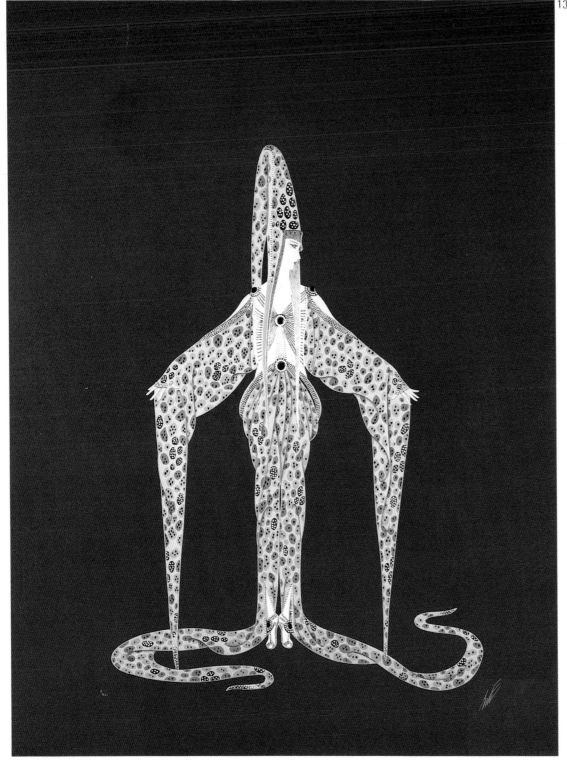

139. Starfish/ 1986

140

140. Perfume/1986

141. The Puppet Show/1986

142 . Harmony/1986

143. Tuxedo/1986

144. The Mystery of Courtesan/1986
145. The Salon/1986

146. Cosmetics Palette&Brush/1989

147.Cosmetics Palette&Brush/1989

THE SCULPTURE

148. L'Amour/1986

149. Je L'Aime

150. Fantasia/1987

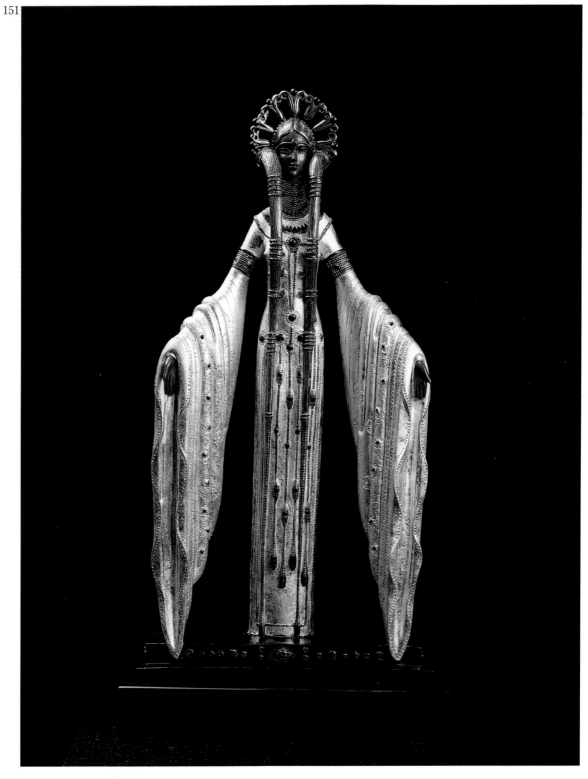

151. Byzantine/1987

152. Triumph/1987

153. Wisdom/1987

154. Beloved/1987

155. Rigolette/1988

156. Love Goddes/1988

157. Emerald Vase/1988

158. Sirens/1988

159. Starstruck/1988

160

161

160. Astra/1988
161. Femme Fatale/1988

162. Dream Birds/1988

163. Venus/1988

164. Pleasure of the Courtesan/1988

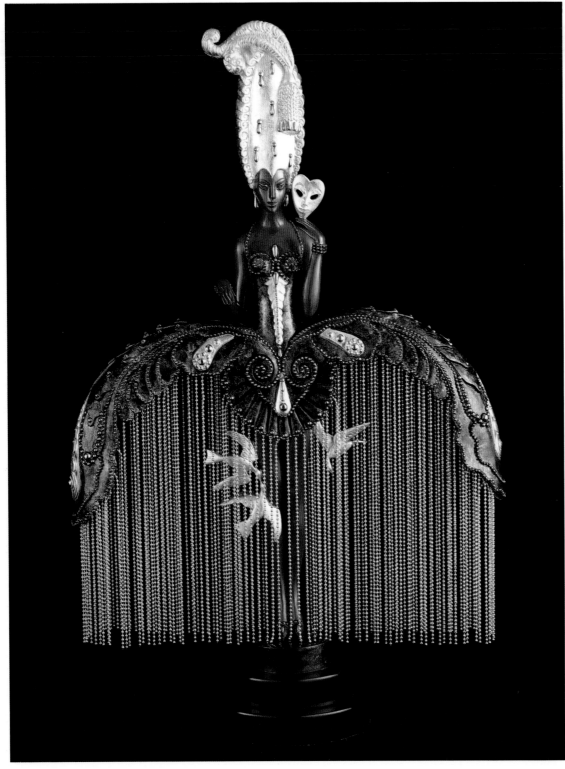

165. Her Secret Admires/1988

166. Heat/1988

167. Feather Gown/1988

168. Lovers&Idol/1988

169. The Slave/1988

170

170. Fireleaves/1989

171. Ecstasy/1989

172. Fedora/1989

THE OBJECTS

173

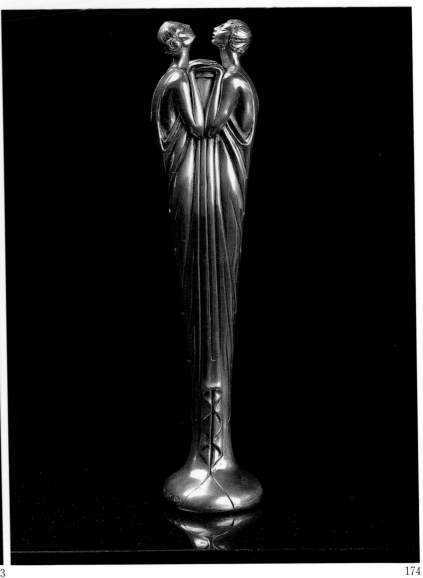

174

173. Flora I
174. Flora II

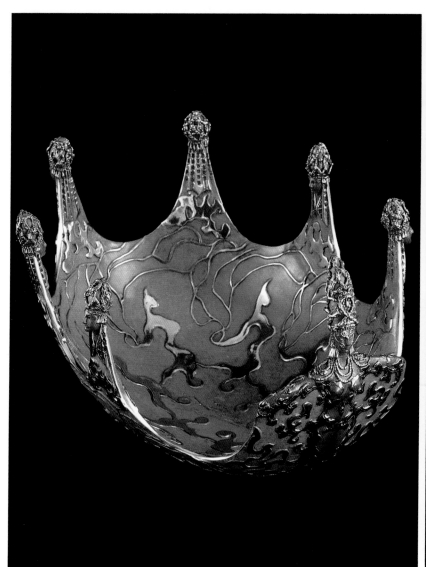

176

175

175.Crapes Flights of Love

176.Ocean II

177

178

177. Vanity
178. Scheherazade

179

180

179. Fruit of Life
180. Style

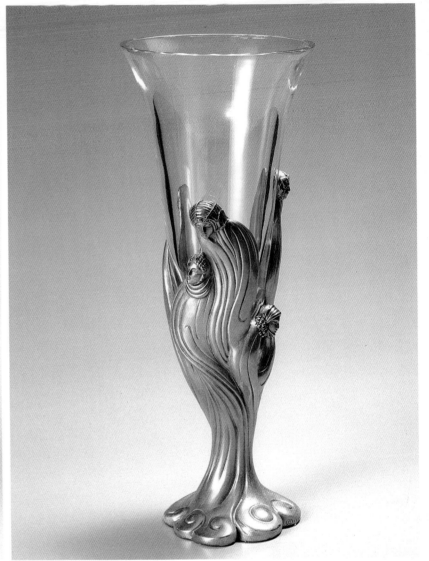

181

182

181. Fantasy
182. Visages de Femme

THE ORIGINAL

211.Golfer(man)/1964

212. Golfer(female)/1964

214. South American(man)/1968

215. South American(female)/1968

183

185

183. Bendel Fashion/1919
185. Manhattan Mary George White Scandals/1927

184

193

184. Robe de Soir/1935
193. Chanteux/1941

213

194

194. Tabac Blond/1941
213. Rahat Lokhoam/1967

197

198

197. Anita/1943
198. Conchita/1943

199

200

199. Nuits du Prologue/1943
200. Chrysis/1943

210

201

192

201. Aisha/1943
192. Keep your hands off/1937
210. Latin Quarter/1961

202. Marriage a Trois Deux du Premier et au cinquieme Tableaux/1944
195. Cadre de Seine Tabarin/1941

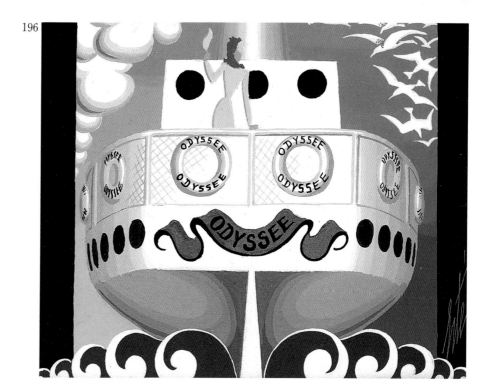

196. La Bateau/1941
203. Musique-Bar Tabarin/1945

204

204. Ace(TRUMP)/1952

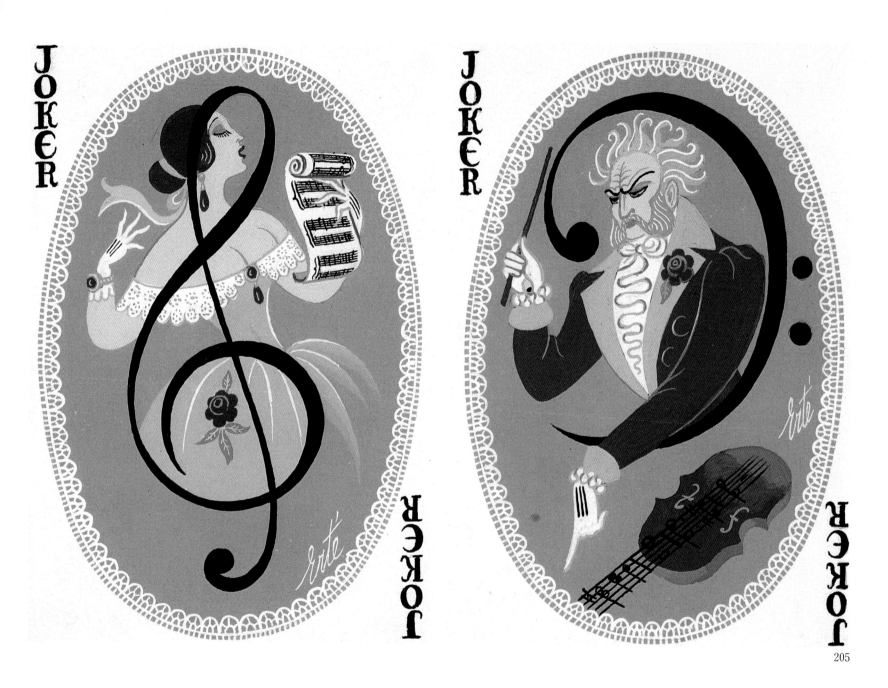

205. Joker(TRUMP)/1952

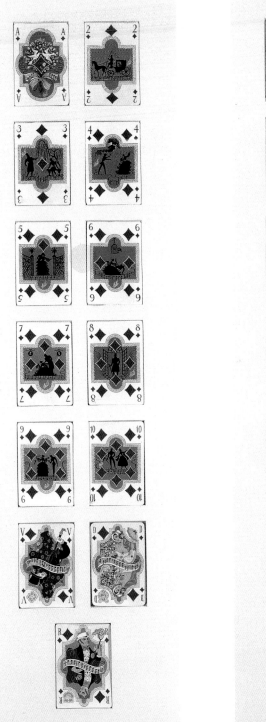

206. Diamond(TRUMP)1952
207. Heart(TRUMP)/1952

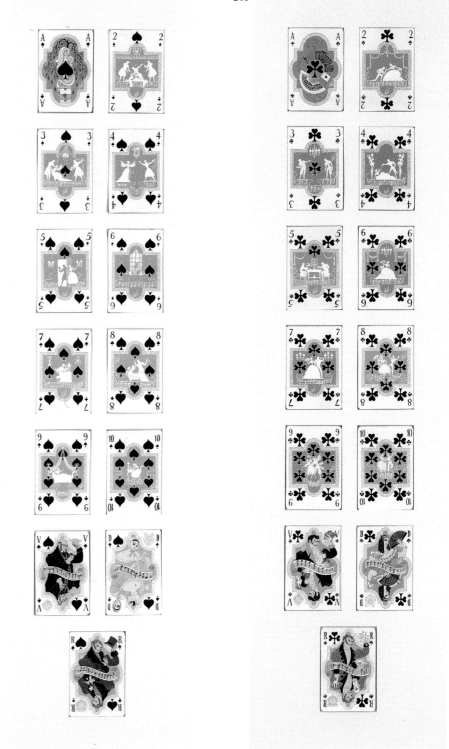

208. Spade(TRUMP)/1952
209. Club(TRUMP)/1952

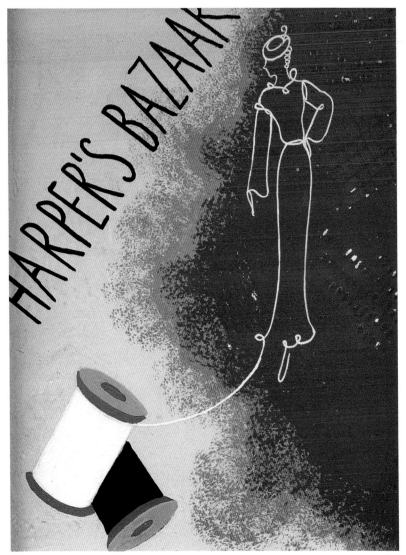

186

187

186. Harper's Bazaar Dress making (№.17181) / 1935
187. Harper's Bazaar Fabrics (№.48) / 1935

188. Harper's Bazaar Bain de Soleil (No.49) / 1935
189. Harper's Bazaar Christmas Present (No.51) / 1935

190. Harper's Bazaar
Merry Christmas/1935

191. Harper's Bazaar
Christmas 1935 (No.9958 A)/1935

L：lithograph S：serigraph E/S：embossed serigraph S/F：serigraph with foil stamping E/S/F：embossed serigraph with foil stamping B：bronze

No. TITLE(series)	MEDIUM	DATE	SIZE(cm)	
〔GRAPHICS〕			sheet size	image size
THE ACES／エースシリーズ				
1.Diamond／ダイヤのエース	L	1974	65.4×49.5	47×33.7
2.Heart／ハートのエース	L	1974	65.4×49.5	47×33.7
3.Spade／スペードのエース	L	1974	65.4×49.5	47×33.7
4.Club／クラブのエース	L	1974	65.4×49.5	47×33.7
THE NUMERALS／数字シリーズ				
5.「0」	E/S	1980	57.2×43.8	42.5×31.8
6.「1」	E/S	1980	57.2×43.8	43.2×31.1
7.「2」	E/S	1980	57.2×43.8	42.5×31.3
8.「3」	E/S	1980	57.2×43.8	40.6×28.6
9.「4」	E/S	1980	57.2×43.8	41.9×30.5
10.「5」	E/S	1980	57.2×43.8	41.9×29.2
11.「6」	E/S	1980	57.2×43.8	40.6×29.2
12.「7」	E/S	1980	57.2×43.8	41.9×29.8
13.「8」	E/S	1980	57.2×43.8	40.6×30.5
14.「9」	E/S	1980	57.2×43.8	41.9×30.5
THE ALRHABET／アルファベットシリーズ				
15.「A」	L/S	1976	64.8×47.9	40×26.7
16.「B」	L/S	1976	64.8×47.9	40×26.7
17.「C」	L/S	1976	64.8×47.9	40×26.7
18.「D」	L/S	1976	64.8×47.9	40×26.7
19.「E」	L/S	1976	64.8×47.9	40×26.7
20.「F」	L/S	1976	64.8×47.9	40×26.7
21.「G」	L/S	1976	64.8×47.9	40×26.7
22.「H」	L/S	1976	64.8×47.9	40×26.7
23.「I」	L/S	1976	64.8×47.9	40×26.7
24.「J」	L/S	1976	64.8×47.9	40×26.7
25.「K」	L/S	1977	64.8×47.9	40×26.7
26.「L」	L/S	1977	64.8×47.9	40×26.7
27.「M」	L/S	1977	64.8×47.9	40×26.7
28.「N」	L/S	1977	64.8×47.9	40×26.7
29.「O」	L/S	1976	64.8×47.9	40×26.7

No. TITLE(series)	MEDIUM	DATE	SIZE(cm)	
30.「P」	L/S	1977	64.8×47.9	40×26.7
31.「Q」	L/S	1977	64.8×47.9	40×26.7
32.「R」	L/S	1977	64.8×47.9	40×26.7
33.「S」	L/S	1977	64.8×47.9	40×26.7
34.「T」	L/S	1977	64.8×47.9	40×26.7
35.「U」	L/S	1977	64.8×47.9	40×26.7
36.「V」	L/S	1977	64.8×47.9	40×26.7
37.「W」	L/S	1977	64.8×47.9	40×26.7
38.「X」	L/S	1977	64.8×47.9	40×26.7
39.「Y」	L/S	1977	64.8×47.9	40×26.7
40.「Z」	L/S	1977	64.8×47.9	40×26.7
VANPS／妖しい女シリーズ				
41. La Pretentieuse／気取った女	L	1979	52.1×38.8	38.1×26.7
42. Black Magic／黒魔術	L	1979	52.1×38.8	38.1×26
43. Circe／魔女キルケ	L	1979	52.1×38.8	36.8×21
44. Seductress／誘惑する女	L	1979	52.1×38.8	37.5×22.4
45. L'Empanachée／羽飾りを付けた女	L	1979	52.1×38.7	35.2×17.5
46. Temptress／男を惑わす女	L	1979	52.1×38.7	37.5×15
THE TWENTIES REMEMBERED／思い出の20年代シリーズより				
47. Les Jolies Dames／美しい女たち	S	1977	61×50.8	45.7×34.3
48 Beauty and the Beast／美女と野獣	S	1977	62.5×54.6	45.7×34.6
METROPOLIS SUITE／大都市シリーズ				
49. On the Avenue／オン・ザ・アベニュー	E/S/F	1985	64.1×75.6	
50. Openning Night／オープニングナイト	E/S/F	1985	64.1×75.6	
MORNING, DAY, EVENING, NIGHT, SUITE／モーニング，デイ，イブニング，ナイトシリーズ				
51. Morning, Day／モーニング，デイ	E/S/F	1985	111.8×85.1	
52. Evening, Night／イブニング，ナイト	E/S/F	1985	111.8×85.1	
JUNE BRIDES SUITE／ジューンブライド・スィート				
53. Fringe Gown／フリンジガウン	E/S/F	1985	97.8×76.8	
54. Veil Gown／ベールガウン	E/S/F	1985	97.8×76.8	
55. Manhattan Mary II／マンハッタン メアリー II	L	1979	59.4×42.2	59.4×42.2
56. Manhattan Mary I／マンハッタン メアリー I	L	1979	55.2×43.8	38.7×28.6
57. Manhattan Mary III／マンハッタン メアリー III	E/S	1989		28.5×39

No. TITLE(series)	MEDIUM	DATE	SIZE(cm)	
58. Manhattan Mary IV／マンハッタン メアリー IV	E／S	1989		28.5×39
59. Manhattan Mary V／マンハッタン メアリー V	E／S	1989		28.5×39
MASQUERADE／マスカレード				
60. Masquerade I／マスカレードI	E／S／F	1987	71.8×101.6	
61. Masquerade II／マスカレードII	E／S／F	1987	71.8×101.6	
PARIS DAY AND NIGHT SUITE／パリ・デイ・アンド・ナイト・スィート				
62. Faubourg St.Honre／セント・オノル座	E／S／F	1987	97.8×77.5	
63. Place de l'Opera／オペラ座	E／S／F	1987	106.1×72.4	
THE AMERICAN MILLIONAIRESS SUITE／大富豪のアメリカ女性				
64. Tassel Gown／タッセルガウン	E／S／F	1987	101.6×71.8	
65. Fringe Cape／フリンジケープ	E／S／F	1987	101.6×66.7	
66. Mother of Pearl／真珠の女神	E／S／F	1987	110.5×69.5	
67. Devotion／愛情	E／S	1987	106.1×79.4	
68. Moon Garden／ムーンガーデン	E／S／F	1987	97.8×73.7	
69. A Dream／夢	E／S／F	1987	101.6×75.6	
70. Ermine Brocade／エルミン・ブロケード	E／S／F	1987	102.2×78	
71. Haute Couture／オートクチュール	E／S／F	1987	94.6×69.9	
72. Gara／ガラ	E／S／F	1987	101.6×73.7	
73. The Harvest／収穫	E／S／F	1987	62.5×94.6	
74. Ladies in Waiting／ウェイティング・レディース	E／S／F	1987	99.7×71.1	
75. Arabian Nights／アラビアンナイト	E／S／F	1987	102.9×74.9	
76. The Necklace／ネックレス	E／S／F	1987	79.4×100.3	
77. Bacchante／バカンテ	E／S／F	1987	102.9×72.4	
78. Lilies and Lace／リリー・アンド・レース	E／S／F	1987	103.5×72.4	
79. Black Rose／黒いバラ	S	1975	63.5×49.5	50.8×38.1
80. Yvette／イヴェット	L	1975	41.6×27.3	16.8×6.4
81. Simone／シモーヌ	L	1975	41.6×27.3	16.5×7.6
82. Renée／ルネ	L	1975	41.6×27.3	16.5×6.4
83. Nicole／ニコル	L	1975	41.6×27.3	17.8×6.4
84. Bon Sir／ボンソワール	L	1975	40.6×30.5	26.7×19
85. Premier／プルミエ	L	1975	40.6×30.5	19×26.7
86. The Veil／チュール	L	1975	30.5×22.9	20.3×15.2
87. Feathers／羽飾り	L	1975	30.5×22.9	20.3×15

作品リスト

No.	TITLE(series)	MEDIUM	DATE	SIZE(cm)	
88.	Summer and Winter／夏と冬	L	1975	27.9×31.8	18.4×22.9
89.	The Kiss／口づけ	L	1975	30.5×25.4	20.3×13.5
90.	Ficelle／紐飾り	L	1976	27.9×38.1	12.7×15.2
91.	Fantaisie／ファンタジー	L	1976	38.1×27.9	17.8×15.2
92.	Summer Breeze／夏のそよ風	S	1978	77.5×58.7	67.3×48.3
93.	Flames of Love／恋の炎	S	1978	68.6×53.3	54.9×40.3
94.	Fall／秋	S	1979	76.2×60.3	61×45
95.	The Mirror／鏡	L	1979	50.8×40.6	50.8×40.6
96.	Gaby Deslys／ギャビーデズリー	L	1979	66×51.1	40.6×51.1
97.	The Golden Cloak／黄金のマント	L	1979	61.6×41.9	54×27.3
98.	Dinarzade／ディナルザード	L	1979	40.6×31.8	40.6×31.8
99.	Zobeide／ゾベイド	L	1979	40.6×31.8	40.6×31.8
100.	Bagdad／バグダッド	L	1979	40.6×31.8	40.6×31.8
101.	King's Favorite／王様のお気に入り	L	1979	63.8×49.8	63.8×49.8
102.	Woman and Satyr／女とサチュロス	S	1980	80×58.7	68.6×48.6
103.	Paresseuse／怠惰な女	S	1980	78.7×58.4	64.5×45.7
104.	Vintage／葡萄の収穫	S	1980	78.7×58.4	64.8×45.7
105.	Heat／ほてり	S	1980	74.5×61	63.5×48.3
106.	Michelle／ミシェル	S	1980	74.6×56.2	63.5×46
107.	The Wave／波	E／S／F	1980	27.3×33	24.1×25
108.	Noon／正午	S	1980	34.3×27.9	22.9×22.9
109.	Lady with a Rose／バラを手にする女	S	1980	55.2×41.3	21×10.2
110.	Rain／雨	E／S	1980	24.4×49.5	11.7×38.7
111.	Twin Sisters／双子の姉妹	S	1981	101.6×139.7	86.4×124.5
112.	Ready for the Ball／舞踏会の仕度	S	1981	62.5×48.9	50.2×41.9
113.	Ready for the Ball／舞踏会の仕度	S	1981	62.5×48.9	50.2×41.9
114.	Cloudy Morning／曇り空の朝	S	1981	61.3×41.9	46.7×27.3
115.	The Duel／決闘	S	1981	77.5×57.2	63.5×45.1
116.	The Bubbles／シャボン玉	S	1981	76.2×60.3	63.5×46.7
117.	Gala Performance／特別上演	S	1981	57.8×45.7	46.4×35.6
118.	Applause／拍手喝采	S	1981	72.4×58.1	58.4×45.7
119.	The Coming of Spring／春の訪れ	S	1981	74.5×58.4	62.9×45.7
120.	Ebony and White／エボニー・アンド・ホワイト	S	1982	55.9×76.2	

No.	TITLE(series)	MEDIUM	DATE	SIZE(cm)
121.	The Surprises of the Sea／海からの贈り物	S	1982	83.8×63.5
122.	Writer in Landscape／風景作家	S	1982	76.5×56.5
123.	The Angel／天使	S	1983	67.3×96.5
124.	Columbine／コロンバイン	S	1983	84.5×65.4
125.	The Clasp／ザ・クラスプ	S	1983	108×64.8
126.	Loge de Théâter／桟敷席	E／S／F	1984	83.8×68.6
127.	Moonlight／ムーンライト	S／F	1984	49.5×50.8
128.	Sunrise／夜明け	S／F	1984	33.7×54
129.	Emerald Eyes／エメラル色の瞳	E／S／F	1985	88.9×71.1
130.	Aphrodite／アフロディーテ	E／S／F	1985	101.6×78.1
131.	Feather Gown／フェザーガウン	E／S／F	1985	92.5×70
132.	Pillow Sing／揺り椅子	E／S／F	1985	73×53.3
133.	Rigoletto／リゴレット	E／S／F	1985	96.5×79.4
134.	The Mirror／鏡	E／S／F	1985	73.7×62.9
135.	The Contessa／伯爵夫人	E／S／F	1985	99.4×59.1
136.	Three Ghaces／スリーグレイシィズ	E／S／F	1985	83.8×62.9
137.	The Pursuite of Flore／フローラを追いかけて	E／S／F	1985	83.8×67.3
138.	Glamour／魅力	E／S／F	1985	56.5×52.7
139.	Starfish／スターフィシュ	E／S／F	1986	99.7×31.8
140.	Perfume／香水	E／S／F	1986	101.6×59.7
141.	The Puppet Show／人形劇	E／S／F	1986	73.7×52.7
142.	Harmony／ハーモニー	E／S／F	1986	83.8×70.5
143.	Tuxedo／タキシード	E／S／F	1986	78.1×55.9
144.	The Mystery of the Courtesan／ミステリー	E／S／F	1986	66×79.4
145.	The Salon／サロン	E／S／F	1986	55.3×74.3
146.	Cosmetics Palette & Brush／コスメティックス・パレット・アンド・ブラシ	E／S	1989	
147.	Cosmetics Palette & Brush／コスメティックス・パレット・アンド・ブラシ	E／S	1989	
〔SCULPTURE〕				(hight)
148.	L'Amour		1986	H 54
149.	Je L'Aime	B		H 38
150.	Fantasia	B	1987	H 53
151.	Byzantine	B	1987	H 51
152.	Triumph	B	1987	H 55

No.	TITLE(series)	MEDIUM	DATE	SIZE(cm)
153.	Wisdom	B	1987	H 41
154.	Beloved	B	1987	H 44
155.	Rigolette	B	1988	H 45
156.	Love Goddes	B	1988	H 50
157.	Emerald Vase	B	1988	H 60
158.	Sirens	B	1988	H 30
159.	Starstruck	B	1988	H 56
160.	Astra	B	1988	H 48
161.	Femme Fatale	B	1988	H 52
162.	Dream Birds	B	1988	H 46
163.	Venus	B	1988	H 60
164.	Pleasure of the Courtesan	B	1988	H 48
165.	Her Secret Admires	B	1988	H 61
166.	Heat	B	1988	H 50
167.	Feather Gown	B	1988	H 44
168.	Lovers & Idol	B	1988	H 51
169.	The Slave	B	1988	H 47
170.	Fireleaves	B	1989	H 48
171.	Ecstasy	B	1989	H 51
172.	Fedora	B	1989	H 48
〔OBJECTS〕				
173.	Flora Ⅰ			H 35.2
174.	Flora Ⅱ			H 35.2
175.	Grapes Flights of Love			H 43.2
176.	Ocean Ⅱ			H 20
177.	Vanity			H 31.6
178.	Scheherazade			H 75.6
179.	Fruit of Life			H 22.2
180.	Style			H 32.4
181.	Fantasy			H 35.6
182.	Visages de Femme			H 34.9
〔ORIGINAL GRAPHICS〕〕				(frame size)
183.	Bendel Fashion	Gouache	1919	44×40.5

No. TITLE(series)	MEDIUM	DATE	SIZE(cm)
184. Robe de Soir	Gouache	1927	56.5 × 43.5
185. Manhattan Mary George White Scandals	Gouache	1925	77.5 × 71.5
186. Harper's Bazaar Dress making (No.17181)	Gouache	1935	62 × 54
187. Harper's Bazaar Fabrics (No.48)	Gouache	1935	62 × 54
188. Harper's Bazaar Bain de Soleil (No.49)	Gouache	1935	62 × 54
189. Harper's Bazaar Christmas Present (No.51)	Gouache	1935	62 × 54
190. Harper's Bazaar Merry Christmas	Gouache	1935	62 × 54
191. Harper's Bazaar Christmas 1935 (No.9958A)	Gouache	1935	62 × 54
192. Keep your hands off	Gouache	1937	
193. Chanteux	Gouache	1941	56.5 × 43.5
194. Tabac Blond	Gouache	1941	56.5 × 43.5
195. Cadre de Seine Tabarin	Gouache	1941	59 × 77
196. La Bateau	Gouache	1941	36.5 × 38
197. Anita	Gouache	1943	56.5 × 43.5
198. Conchita	Gouache	1943	56.5 × 43.5
199. Nuits du Prologue	Gouache	1943	56.5 × 43.5
200. Chrysis	Gouache	1943	56.5 × 43.5
201. Aisha	Gouache	1943	56.5 × 43.5
202. Marriage a Trois Deux du Premier et au cinquieme Tableaux	Gouache	1944	60 × 66
203. Musique-Bar Tabarin	Gouache	1945	63 × 59.5
204. Ace (TRUMP)	Gouache	1952	32 × 39.5
205. Joker (TRUMP)	Gouache	1952	32 × 39.5
206. Diamond (TRUMP)	Gouache	1952	133 × 39.5
207. Heart (TRUMP)	Gouache	1952	133 × 39.5
208. Spade (TRUMP)	Gouache	1952	133 × 39.5
209. Club (TRUMP)	Gouache	1952	133 × 39.5
210. Latin Quarter	Gouache	1961	63.5 × 68
211. Golfer (man)	Gouache	1964	53.5 × 42.5
212. Golfer (female)	Gouache	1964	53.5 × 42.5
213. Rahat Lokhoam	Gouache	1967	
214. South American (man)	Gouache	1968	53.5 × 42.5
215. South American (female)	Gouache	1968	53.5 × 42.5

ERTÉ
"LEADER OF ART DECO HIS TRAIL THROUGH THE CENTURY"
Editorial Staff: GAP JAPAN Co., Ltd.
                Sevenarts Tokyo the ERTÉ Gallery
Publisher: Yoshiaki Yanada
Published by: JAPAN PLANNING ASSOCIATION Co.,Ltd.
Printed in Japan, 1990